TREASURY OF PATCHWORK QUILT SETS

Elizabeth F. Nyhan

DOVER PUBLICATIONS, INC.
New York

Published in Canada by General Publishing Company, Ltd., 30 Lesmill Road, Don Mills, Toronto, Ontario.
Published in the United Kingdom by Constable and Company, Ltd., 3 The Lanchesters, 162–164 Fulham Palace Road, London W6 9ER.

Bibliographical Note

Treasury of Patchwork Quilt Sets is a new work, first published by Dover Publications, Inc., in 1994.

Library of Congress Cataloging-in-Publication Data

Nyhan, Elizabeth F.
   Treasury of patchwork quilt sets / Elizabeth F. Nyhan.
      p.   cm.
   ISBN 0-486-28148-5
   1. Patchwork—Patterns 2. Quilting—Patterns. I. Title.
TT835.N96 1994
746.9'7041—dc20
                                                     94-17258
                                                   CIP

Manufactured in the United States of America
Dover Publications, Inc., 31 East 2nd Street, Mineola, N.Y. 11501

INTRODUCTION

To a very large extent, it is the way that colors and tones are arranged within a quilt that give it its character. The creative potential of any given quilt design is almost limitless. Not only are there a large number of variations possible within a single block, but the arrangement of the blocks themselves (called the "quilt set") further multiplies the design possibilities.

It is this myriad of possibilities that make quilting so exciting. At the same time, however, this freedom can be daunting.

If you have ever designed a quilt, you know that it can be a time-consuming process—even before you cut your fabric. First you must draw the quilt on graph paper—as many blocks as possible. Then you begin experimenting with the color, pattern and shading of the pieces. A new set of blocks must be drawn for each variation, since a block that looks great by itself may not give you the effect you want when it is expanded to a full-size quilt. In addition to taking a lot of time, this process is prone to error—you might make a mistake in drawing the lines of the basic design, or you might color in the wrong piece or use the wrong color on a piece. These mistakes can lead to a lot of erasing, redrawing and frustration.

The purpose of this book is twofold—to reduce the redrawing necessary and ease some of the quilter's frustration during the design phase and to give the quilt designer some new ideas as to color and pattern placement.

The book presents ten different quilt blocks based on the basic Nine Patch design. Full-size pattern pieces to make each block in each of three different sizes—6″ square, 9″ square and 12″ square—are included on the last two pages of the book. Each of the ten blocks is presented in the same way. First, a full-size drawing (6″ size) of the block is shown. Below this are a number of possible color variations of the block. The pattern pieces needed to create the block are listed next. On the following page, or pages, simple line drawings of possible quilt sets are given. At least two set variations are given for each quilt—the basic set with the blocks placed side by side, and a set showing every other block blank. If different effects can be created by rotating the block, these variations will be shown next. These drawings can be used for coloring and planning your own quilt and I suggest making photocopies of them.

Next, the set variations are shown. A short description is given with each set variation, explaining which block variations are used and whether an odd or even number of rows is required to make the design symmetrical. Unless an even number of rows is required for symmetry, each set variation shows five by seven rows of blocks.

At the end of the book, you will find the full-size pattern pieces needed to make the quilts shown. In order to save room, all three sizes of each pattern piece are shown together, one inside the other, each one marked with the block size. To use the patterns, trace the desired size onto translucent plastic or onto paper. Glue the paper to lightweight cardboard. In order to avoid confusion, seam allowances have *not* been added to the pieces, so, if you are planning to sew the pieces together by machine, add ¼″ around each piece now. If you are planning to sew the pieces together by hand, it is not necessary to add the seam allowance to the templates. Cut out the templates.

To use the templates, trace them to the wrong side of the fabric, placing the arrows on the lengthwise or crosswise grain, and being sure to allow room for seam allowances on pieces for hand sewing. Cut out the pieces. When cutting out pieces for hand sewing, be sure to cut ¼″ outside of the traced line.

Sew all pieces with right sides together. For hand sewing, match the traced seamlines, and sew exactly on the line, starting and stopping exactly on the ends of the line. For machine sewing, use the cut edge of the fabric as a guide for the presser foot. Press all seams to one side.

BLOCK I
Basic Nine Patch

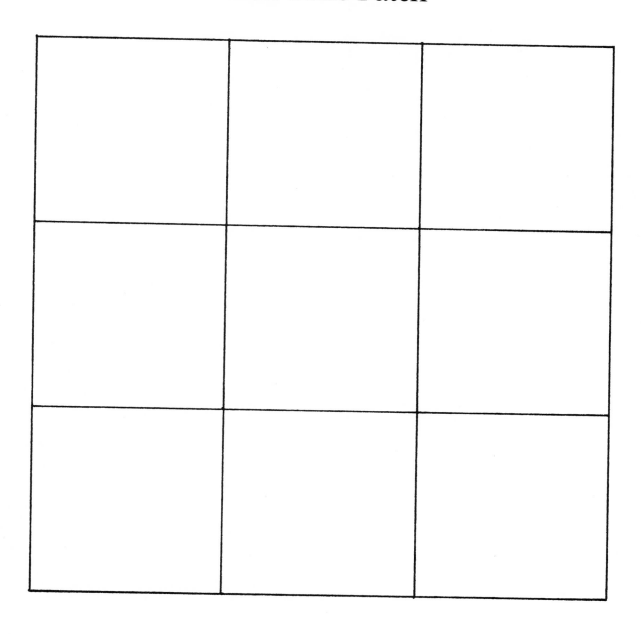

1   2   3

Block variations

Pattern pieces required: A

Block I—Blank set drawings

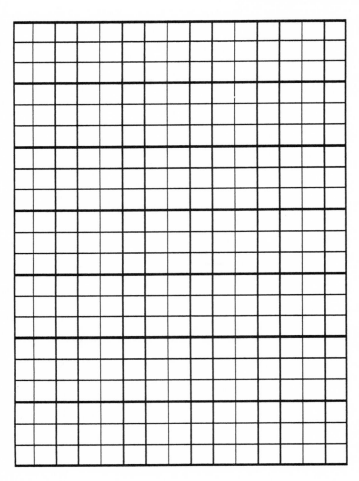

Basic set.

Every other block blank. An odd number of horizontal and vertical rows is required for symmetry.

Block I—Set variations

Blocks with dark centers and corners/light sides, alternating with blocks with light centers and corners/medium sides. An odd number of horizontal and vertical rows is required for symmetry.
Blocks 1 and 3

Alternating dark and medium blocks. An odd number of horizontal and vertical rows is required for symmetry.
Blocks 1 and 2

Block I—Set variations

Every other block blank. An odd number of horizontal and vertical rows is required for symmetry.
Block 1

BLOCK II

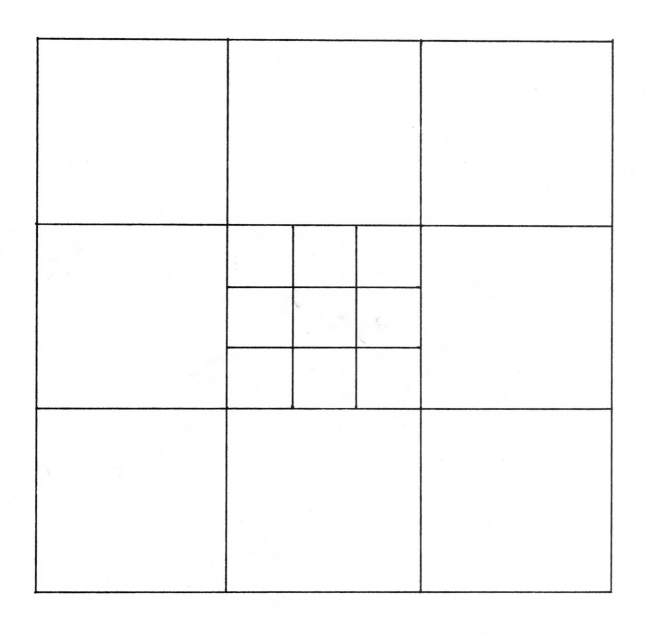

1   2   3   4   5   6

Block variations

Pattern pieces required: A, E

Block II—Blank set drawings

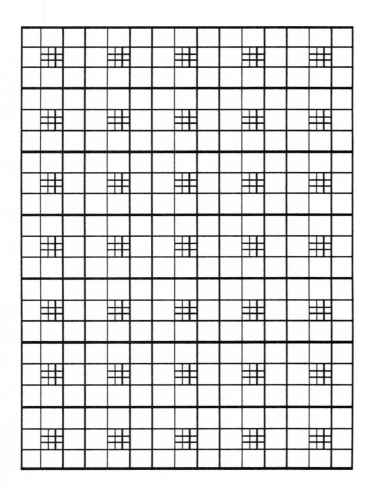

Basic set.

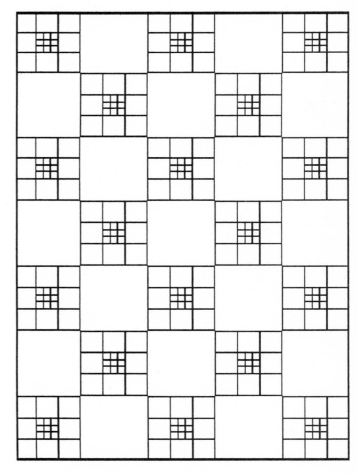

Every other block blank. An odd number of horizontal and vertical rows is required for symmetry.

Block II—Set variations

Dark blocks.
Block 1

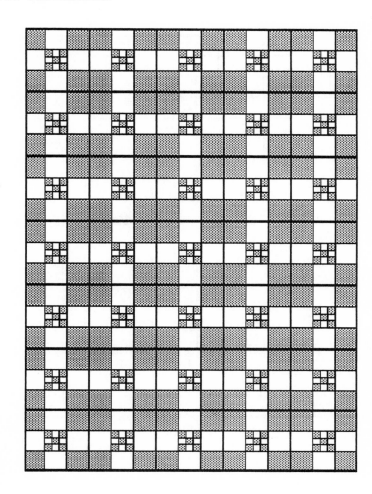

Dark blocks alternating with medium blocks.
An odd number of horizontal and vertical rows
is required for symmetry.
Blocks 1 and 4

Block II—Set variations

Blocks with dark corners and light sides alternating with blocks with light corners and medium sides. An odd number of horizontal and vertical rows is required for symmetry.
Blocks 1 and 3

Blocks with dark sides alternating with blocks with medium sides and very dark centers. An odd number of horizontal and vertical rows is required for symmetry.
Blocks 2 and 5

Block II—Set variations

Blocks with medium corners and very dark centers.
Block 6

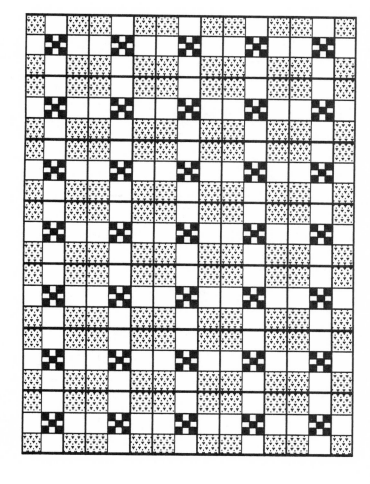

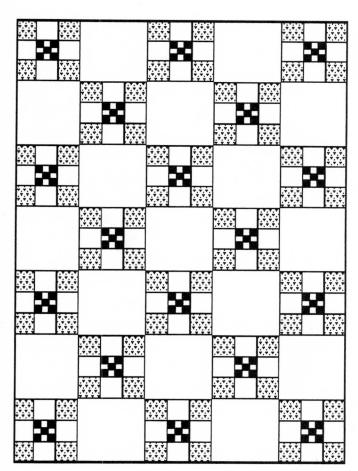

Every other block blank. An odd number of horizontal and vertical rows is required for symmetry.
Block 6

BLOCK III

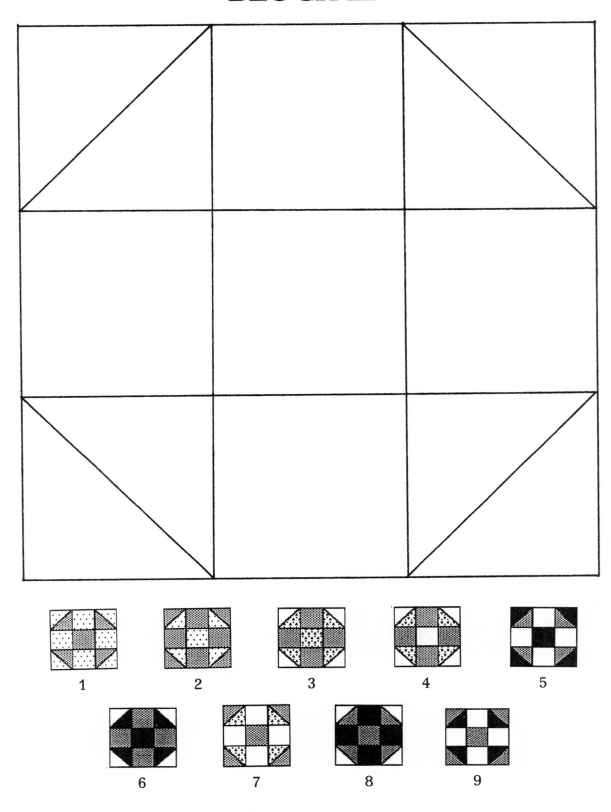

Block variations

Pattern pieces required: A, B

14

Block III—Blank set drawings

Basic set.

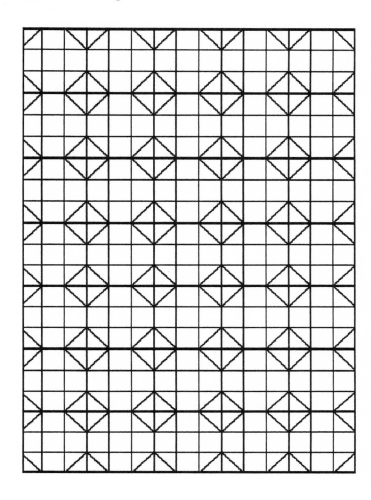

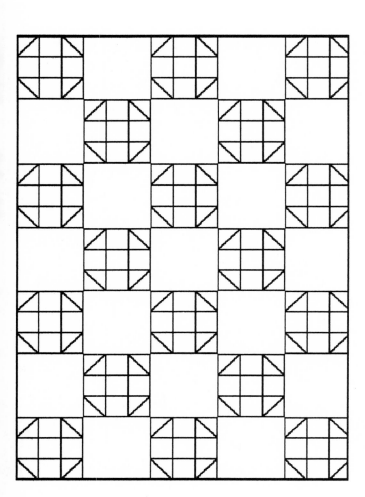

Every other block blank. An odd number of horizontal and vertical rows is required for symmetry.

Block III—Set variations

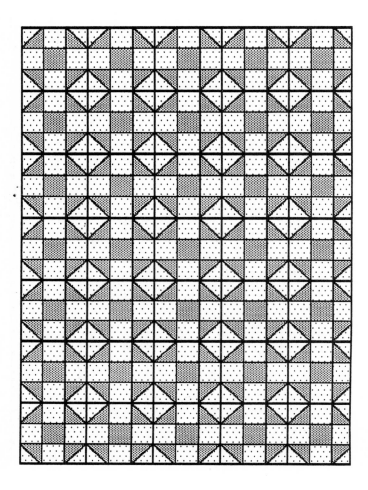

Light background, dark design.
Block 1

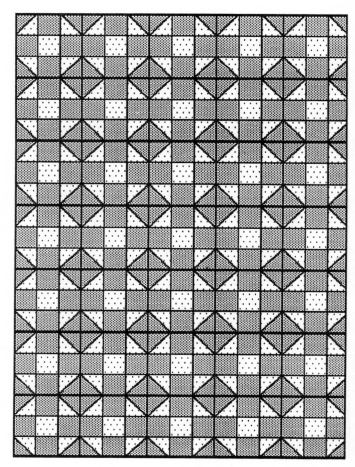

Dark background, light design.
Block 2

Block III—Set variations

Medium inside triangles, dark sides, light centers and corners.
Block 4

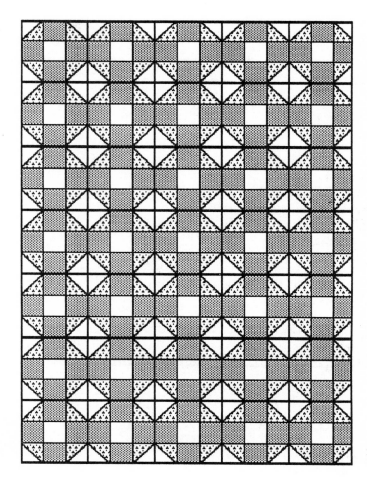

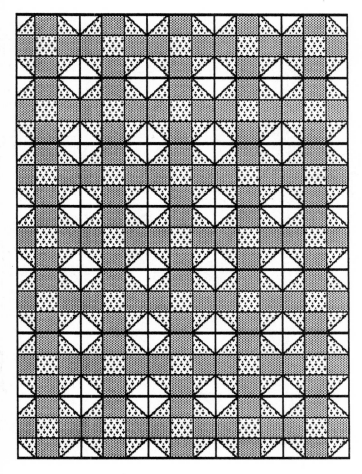

Medium inside triangles and centers, dark sides.
Block 3

Block III—Set variations

Alternating dark and light backgrounds. An odd number of horizontal and vertical rows is required for symmetry.
Blocks 1 and 2

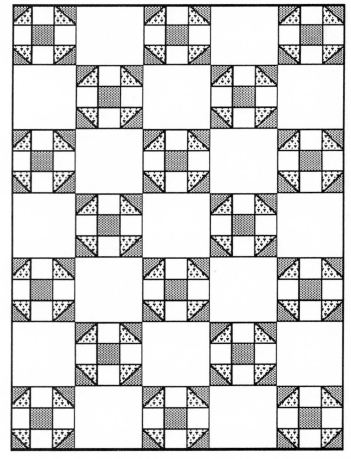

Every other block blank. An odd number of horizontal and vertical rows is required for symmetry.
Block 7

Block III—Set variations

Blocks with dark sides and very dark inside triangles and centers, alternating with blocks with very dark sides and dark inside triangles and centers. An odd number of horizontal and vertical rows is required for symmetry.
Blocks 6 and 8

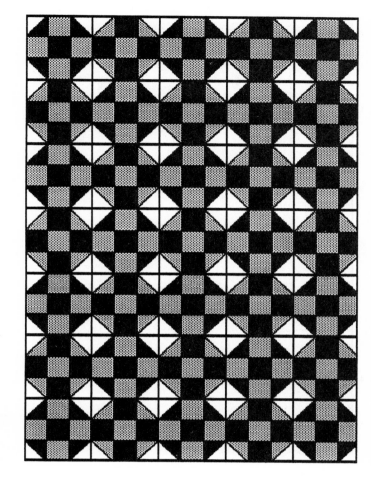

Blocks with dark inside triangles and very dark corners and centers, alternating with blocks with very dark inside triangles and dark corners and centers. An odd number of horizontal and vertical rows is required for symmetry.
Blocks 5 and 9

BLOCK IV

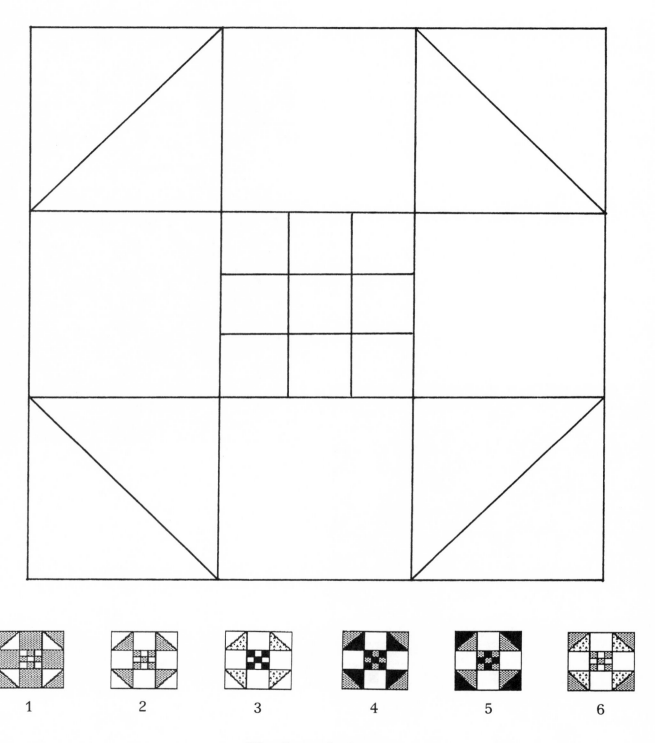

Block variations

Pattern pieces required: A, B, E

Block IV—Blank set drawings

Basic set.

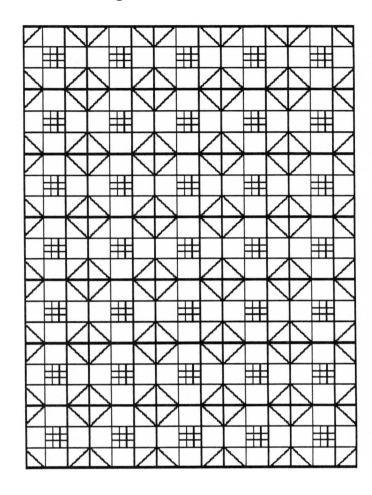

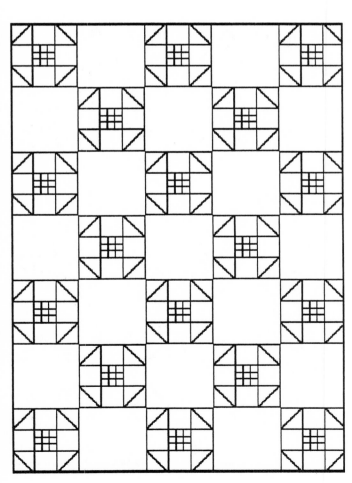

Every other square blank. An odd number of horizontal and vertical rows is required for symmetry.

Block IV—Set variations

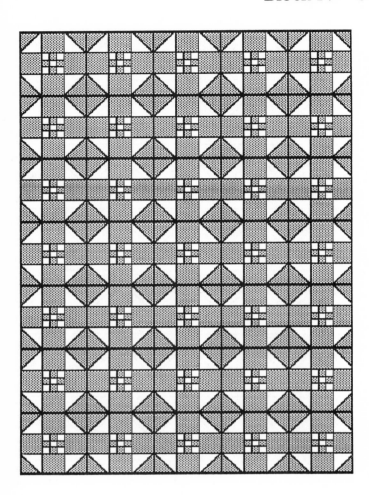

Dark background, light design.
Block 1

Light background, dark design.
Block 2

Block IV—Set variations

Alternating light and dark backgrounds. An odd number of horizontal and vertical rows is required for symmetry.
Blocks 1 and 2

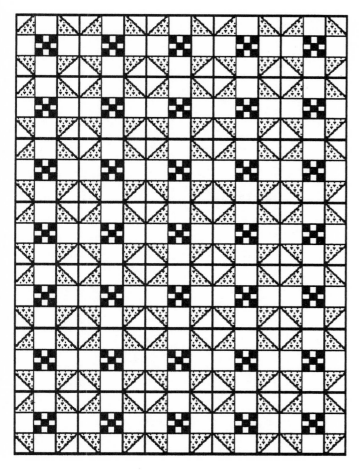

Medium inside triangles, very dark centers.
Block 3

Block IV—Set variations

Dark inside triangles, very dark corners and
light sides.
Block 5

Very dark inside triangles, dark corners and
light sides.
Block 4

Block IV—Set variations

Alternating dark and very dark design. An odd number of horizontal and vertical rows is required for symmetry.
Blocks 4 and 5

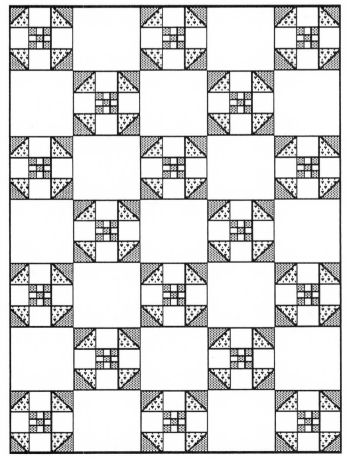

Every other block blank; medium inside triangles, dark corners and light sides. An odd number of horizontal and vertical rows is required for symmetry.
Block 6

BLOCK V

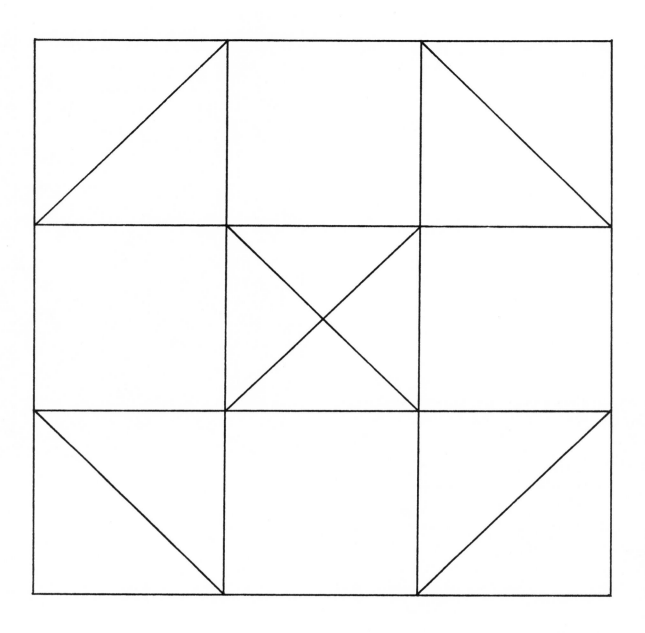

1

2

Block variations

Pattern pieces required: A, B, C

Block V—Blank set drawings

Basic set.

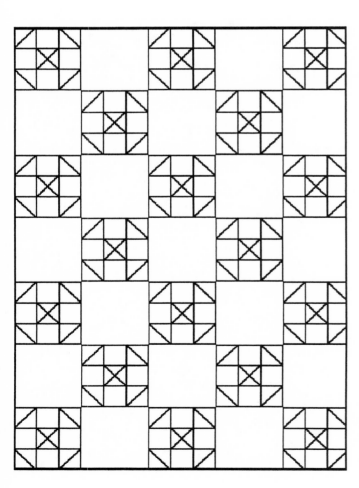

Every other block blank. An odd number of horizontal and vertical rows is required for symmetry.

Block V—Set variations

Dark background, light inside triangles.
Block 1

Light background, dark inside triangles.
Block 2

Block V—Set variations

Alternating dark and light backgrounds. An odd number of horizontal and vertical rows is required for symmetry.
Blocks 1 and 2

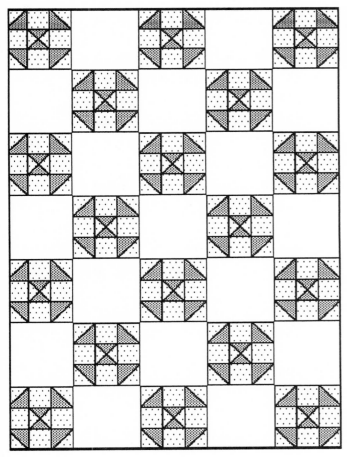

Every other block blank. An odd number of horizontal and vertical rows is required for symmetry.
Block 2

BLOCK VI

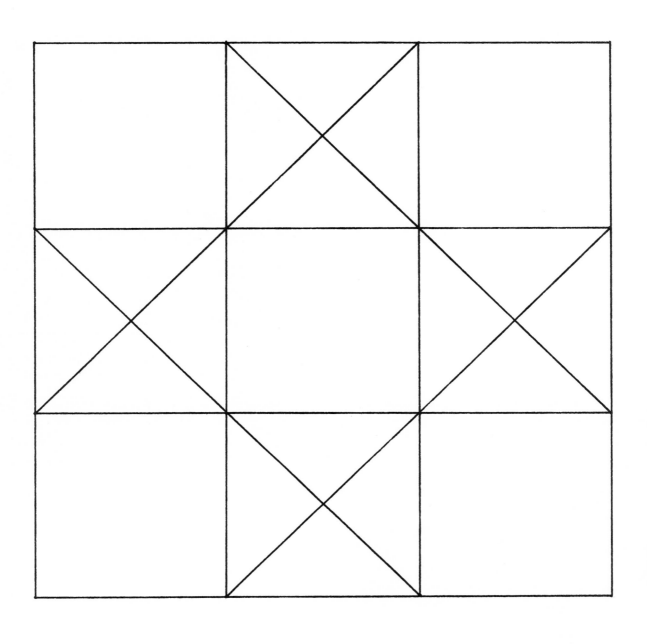

1

2

3

4

5

6

Block variations

Pattern pieces required: A, C

Block VI—Blank set drawings

Basic set.

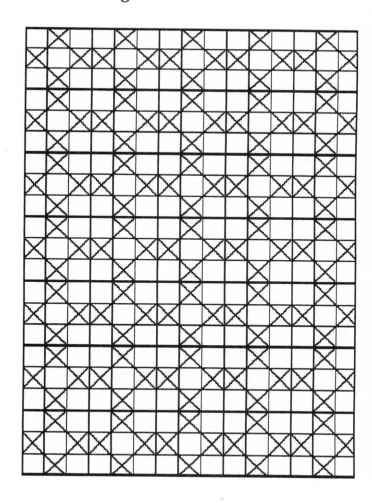

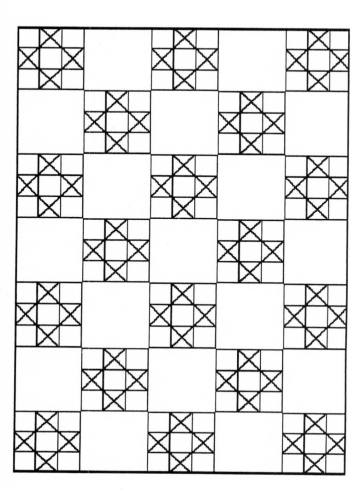

Every other square blank. An odd number of horizontal and vertical rows is required for symmetry.

Block VI—Set variations

Light background, dark design.
Block 1

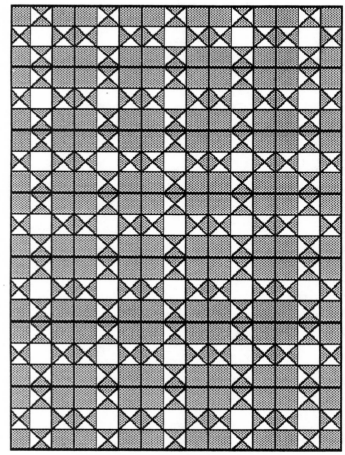

Dark background, light design.
Block 2

Block VI—Set variations

Alternating dark and light backgrounds. An odd number of horizontal and vertical rows is required for symmetry.
Blocks 1 and 2

Every other square blank. An odd number of horizontal and vertical rows is required for symmetry.
Block 4

Block VI—Set variations

Dark design with very dark inside triangles.
Block 3

Dark inside triangles, very dark center squares.
Block 5

Block VI—Set variations

Dark triangles, light background.
Block 6

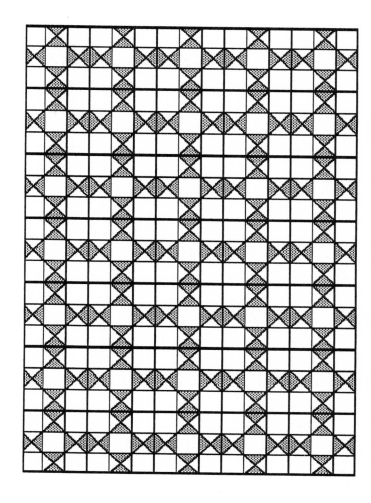

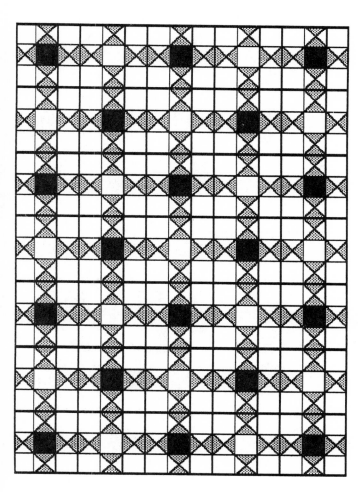

Dark triangles, alternating very dark and light centers. An odd number of horizontal and vertical rows is required for symmetry.
Blocks 5 and 6

BLOCK VII

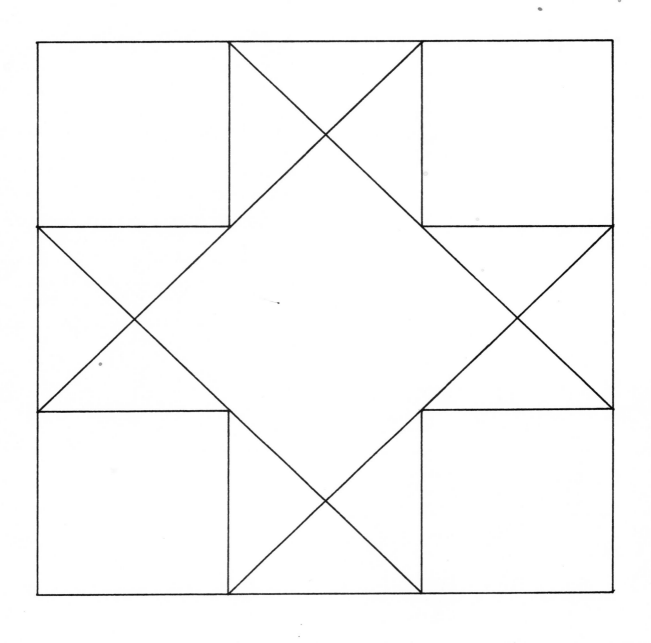

1   2   3   4   5   6   7

Block variations

Pattern pieces required: A, C, D

Block VII—Blank set drawings

Basic set.

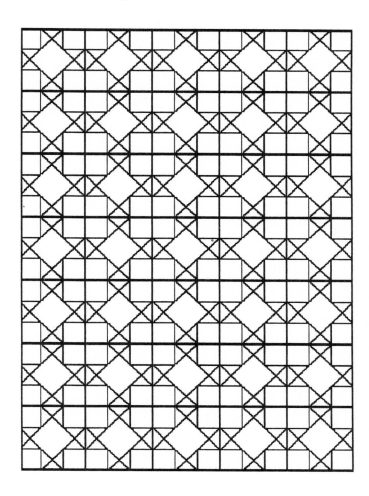

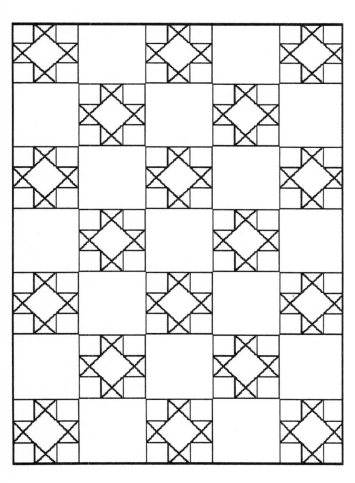

Every other square blank. An odd number of horizontal and vertical rows is required for symmetry.

Block VII—Set variations

Light background, dark design.
Block 1

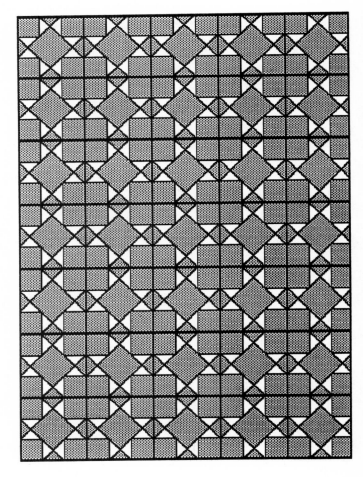

Dark background, light design.
Block 2

Block VII—Set variations

Alternating light and dark backgrounds. An odd number of horizontal and vertical rows is required for symmetry.
Blocks 1 and 2

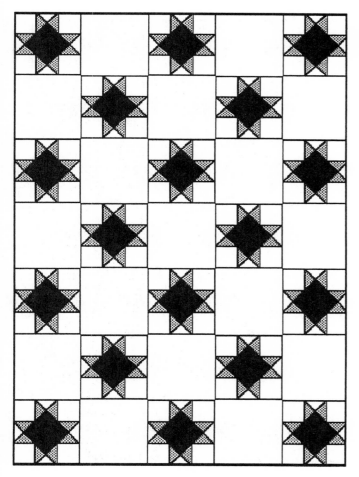

Every other square blank. An odd number of horizontal and vertical rows is required for symmetry.
Block 4

Block VII—Set variations

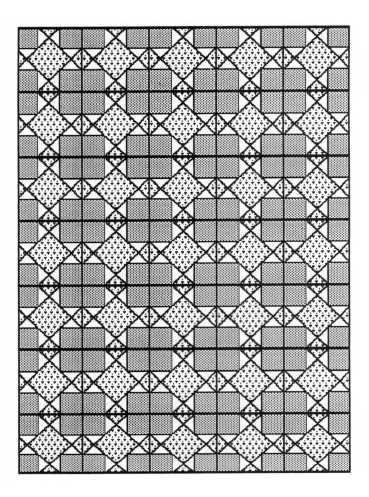

Dark background, light inside triangles, medium sides and centers.
Block 5

Light background, medium inside triangles, dark sides and centers.
Block 6

Block VII—Set variations

Dark inside triangles and light corners, alternating very dark and light centers. An odd number of horizontal and vertical rows is required for symmetry.
Blocks 3 and 4

Dark and very dark inside triangles, medium centers, light corners.
Block 7

BLOCK VIII

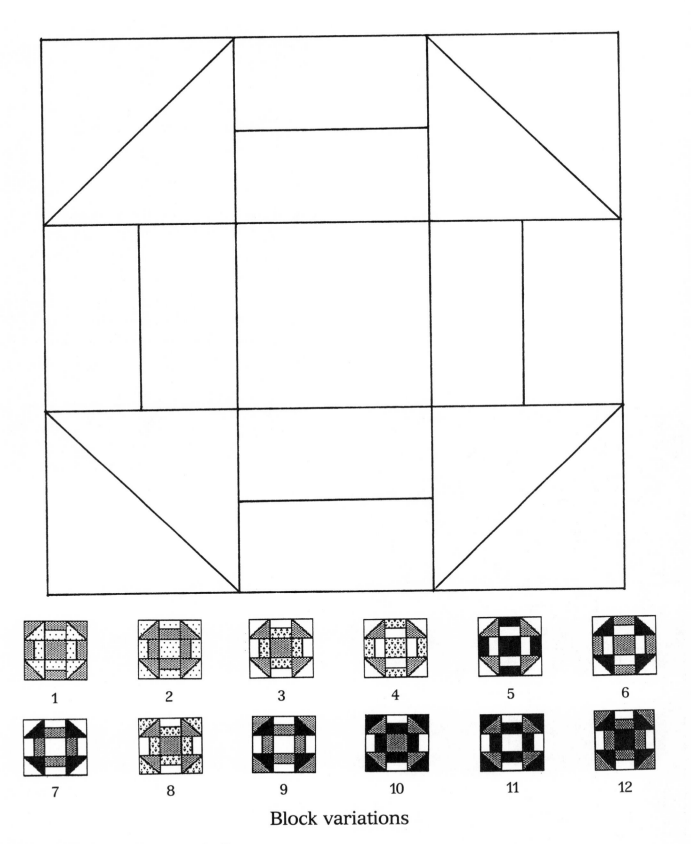

Block variations

Pattern pieces required: A, B, F

Block VIII—Blank set drawings

Basic set.

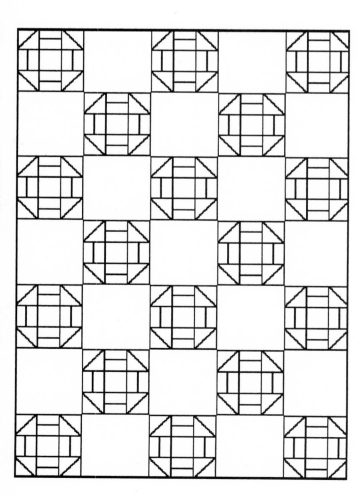

Every other square blank. An odd number of horizontal and vertical rows is required for symmetry.

Block VIII—Set variations

Dark background, light design.
Block 1

Light background, dark design.
Block 2

Block VIII—Set variations

Alternating dark and light backgrounds. An odd number of horizontal and vertical rows is required for symmetry.
Blocks 1 and 2

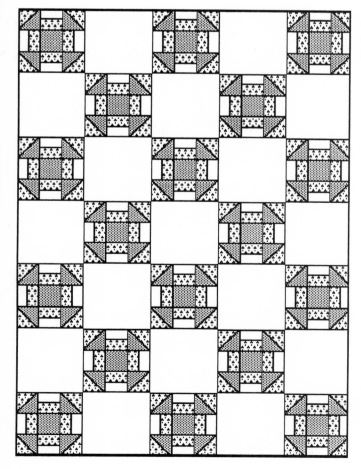

Every other square blank. An odd number of horizontal and vertical rows is required for symmetry.
Block 8

Block VIII—Set variations

Dark inner triangles and centers, medium inner rectangles, light background.
Block 3

Very dark inner triangles, dark inner triangles, light background.
Block 7

Block VIII—Set variations

Blocks with very dark inner triangles, dark centers and outer rectangles alternating with blocks with dark inner triangles, very dark centers and outer rectangles. An odd number of horizontal and vertical rows is required for symmetry.
Blocks 5 and 6

Dark inner triangles, medium outer rectangles and centers, light inner rectangles and corners.
Block 4

Block VIII—Set variations

Blocks with dark inner triangles and very dark corners alternating with blocks with very dark inner triangles and dark corners. An odd number of horizontal and vertical rows is required for symmetry.
Blocks 9 and 11

Blocks with dark inner triangles and centers alternating with blocks with very dark inner triangles and centers. An odd number of horizontal and vertical rows is required for symmetry.
Blocks 10 and 12

BLOCK IX

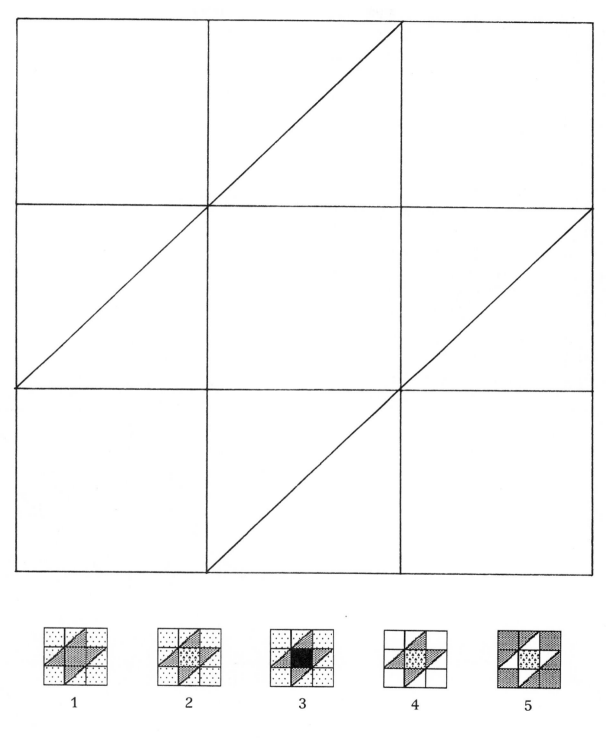

Block variations

Pattern pieces required: A, B

Block IX—Blank set drawings

Basic set.

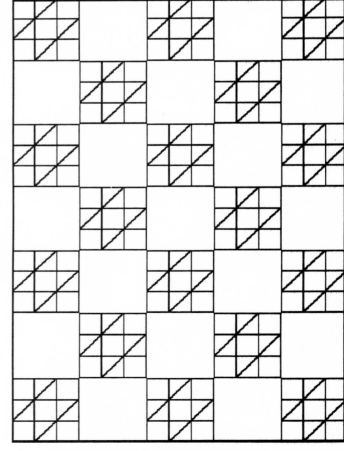

Every other block blank. An odd number of horizontal and vertical rows is required for symmetry.

Block IX—Blank set drawings

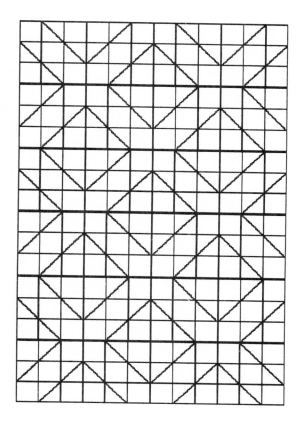

Four-block main design, pointing outward. An even number of horizontal and vertical rows is required for symmetry.

Four-block main design, pointing inward. An even number of horizontal and vertical rows is required for symmetry.

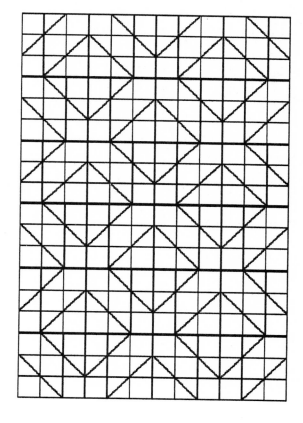

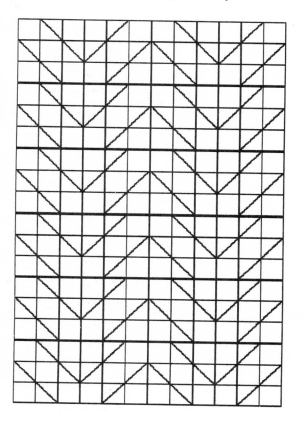

Blocks in vertical rows pointing in the same direction. Rows alternate directions. An even number of vertical rows is required for symmetry.

Block IX—Set variations

Light background, dark design.
Block 1

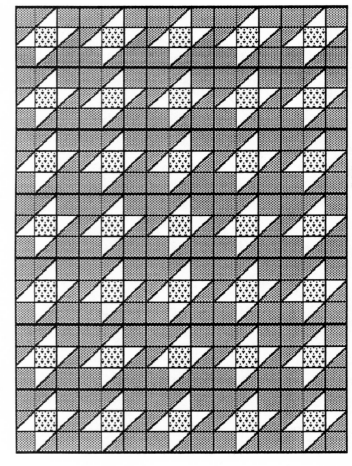

Dark background, light design, medium centers.
Block 5

Block IX—Set variations

Light background, dark design, very dark centers.
Block 3

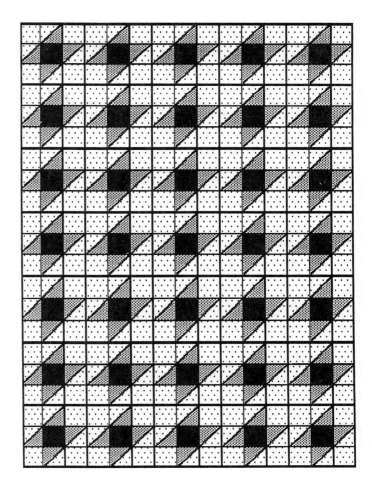

Light background, dark design, medium centers.
Block 4

Block IX—Set variations

Alternating dark and light backgrounds. An odd number of horizontal and vertical rows is required for symmetry.
Blocks 4 and 5

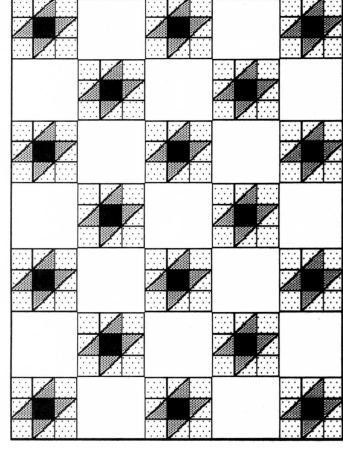

Every other block blank. An odd number of horizontal and vertical rows is required for symmetry.
Block 3

Block IX—Set variations

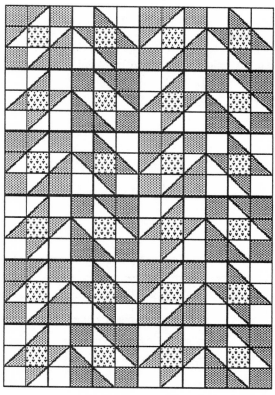

Alternating dark and light backgrounds. Blocks in vertical rows pointing in the same direction. Rows alternate directions. An even number of vertical rows is required for symmetry.
Blocks 4 and 5

Light background, dark design. Four-block design, pointing inward. An even number of horizontal and vertical rows is required for symmetry.
Block 1

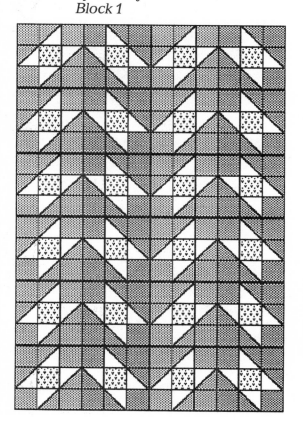

Dark background, light design. Blocks in vertical rows pointing in the same direction. Rows alternate directions. An even number of vertical rows is required for symmetry.
Block 5

Block IX—Set variations

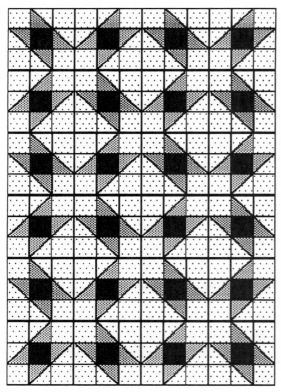

Light background, dark design with very dark centers. Four-block design, pointing outward. An even number of horizontal and vertical rows is required for symmetry.
Block 3

Light background, dark design with medium centers. Four-block design, pointing inward. An even number of horizontal and vertical rows is required for symmetry.
Block 2

Alternating dark and light backgrounds. Four-block design, pointing inward. An even number of horizontal and vertical rows is required for symmetry.
Blocks 4 and 5

BLOCK X

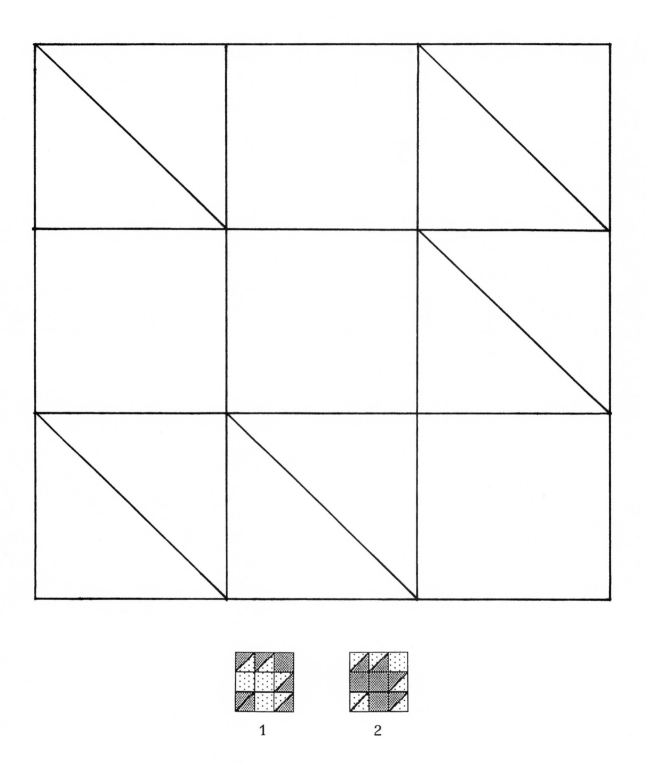

1   2

Block variations

Pattern pieces required: A, B

Block X—Blank set drawings

Basic set.

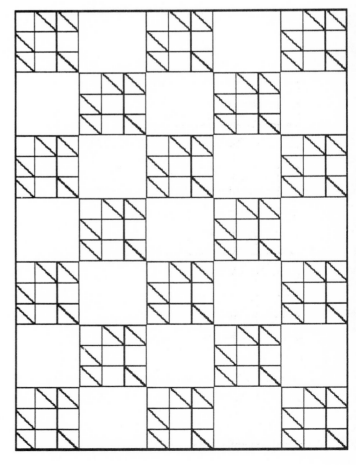

Every other square blank. An odd number of horizontal and vertical rows is required for symmetry.

Block X—Blank set drawings

Four-block main design, pointing outward. An **even number** of horizontal and vertical rows is **required** for symmetry.

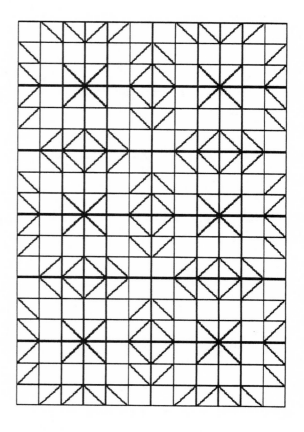

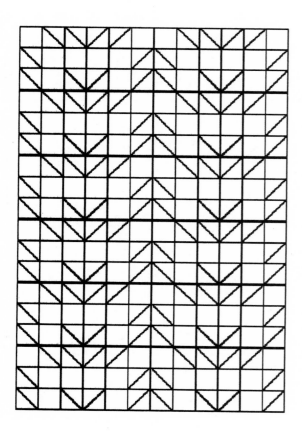

Blocks in vertical rows pointing in the same direction. Vertical rows alternate direction. An even number of vertical rows is required for symmetry.

Block X—Set variations

Dark background, light design.
Block 1

Light background, dark design.
Block 2

Block X—Set variations

Alternating dark and light backgrounds. An odd number of horizontal and vertical rows is required for symmetry.
Blocks 1 and 2

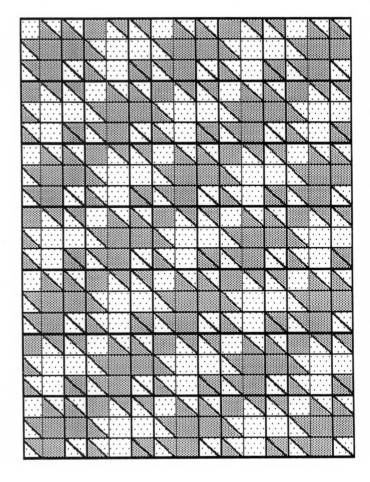

Every other block blank. An odd number of horizontal and vertical rows is required for symmetry.
Block 1

Block X—Set variations

Dark background, light design. Design in vertical rows pointing in the same direction; rows alternate directions. An even number of vertical rows is required for symmetry.
Block 2

Alternating dark and light backgrounds. Four-block design, pointing outward. An even number of horizontal and vertical rows is required for symmetry.
Blocks 1 and 2

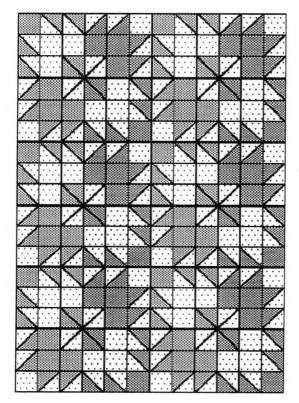

Alternating dark and light backgrounds. Design in vertical rows pointing in the same direction; rows alternate directions. An even number of vertical rows is required for symmetry.
Blocks 1 and 2

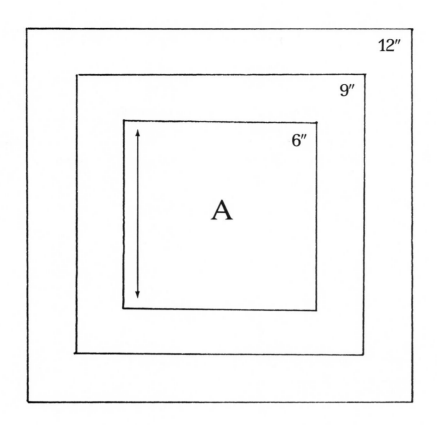

12″

9″

6″

A

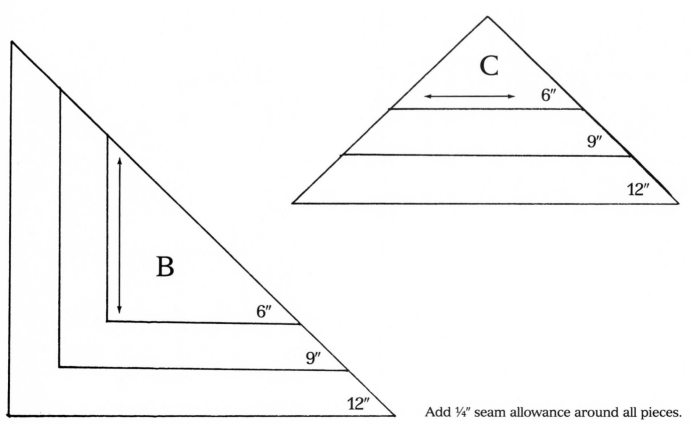

B

6″

9″

12″

C

6″

9″

12″

Add ¼″ seam allowance around all pieces.

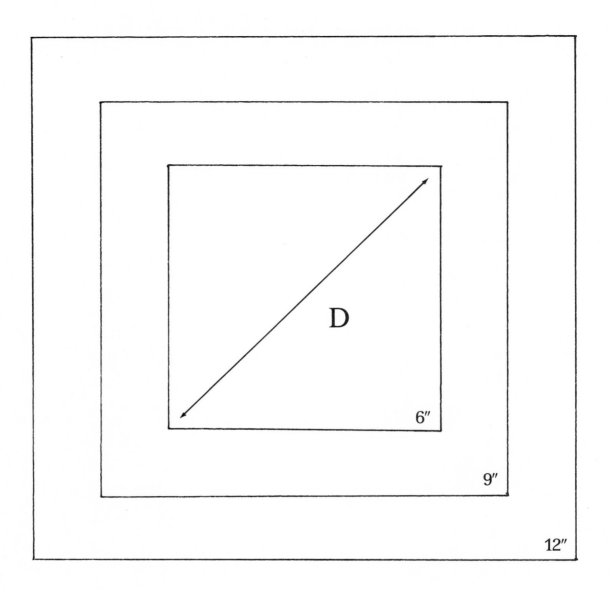

D

6″

9″

12″

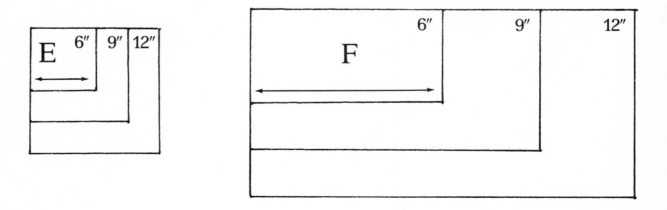

E   6″ 9″ 12″

F   6″   9″   12″

Add ¼″ seam allowance around all pieces.